RUSKIN'S VENICE

Ruskin's Venice

ROBERT HEWISON

Slade Professor of Fine Art
University of Oxford
1999–2000

PILKINGTON PRESS
LONDON

FIRST PUBLISHED 2000
BY PILKINGTON PRESS LTD
YELVERTOFT MANOR
NORTHAMPTONSHIRE NN6 6LF

First published 1978 by Thames and Hudson
as *Ruskin and Venice,* incorporating a catalogue to accompany
an exhibition at the J.B. Speed Art Museum,
Louisville, Kentucky.

ISBN 1 899044 22 1

PRODUCED, DESIGNED AND TYPESET BY:
A.H. JOLLY (EDITORIAL) LTD
YELVERTOFT MANOR
NORTHAMPTONSHIRE NN6 6LF

PRINTED IN GREAT BRITAIN

TITLE PAGE ILLUSTRATION:
George Richmond, *Portrait of John Ruskin at 43.*

CONTENTS

INTRODUCTION

THIS is a revised and enlarged version of the essay that introduced the catalogue of an exhibition, *Ruskin and Venice* which I curated for the J.B. Speed Art Museum, Louisville, Kentucky in 1978, the catalogue being published by Thames and Hudson. My knowledge of both Ruskin and Venice has deepened since then, and there has been the publication of two important books: Van Akin Burd's *John Ruskin and Rose La Touche* (Oxford University Press 1979), which contains important information about Ruskin's mental state during his visit to Venice in 1876–77, and Jeanne Clegg's *Ruskin and Venice* (Junction Books, 1981), which is a comprehensive study of the subject. I gratefully acknowledge the contribution their research has made to my revisions.

I should also like to thank my publisher, Brian Pilkington, for suggesting that the material I had gathered could be republished in a revised version, using additional drawings by Ruskin that had not formed part of the original exhibition catalogue. The essay now stands in its own right, as a tribute to the man whose words and drawings are a priceless record of a place that is beyond price, and whose protective influence, I am glad to say, is still felt in Venice today.

Robert Hewison
The Ruskin Library
University of Lancaster

CHRONOLOGY

1819   John Ruskin born 8 February in London.

1832   Given copy of Roger's *Italy*, with illustrations by Turner.

1833   First family tour abroad, France, Switzerland, and Italy.

1835   Tour of France, Switzerland, and Italy; visits Venice 6–17 October, staying at Hotel Danieli.

1837   Ruskin enters Christ Church, Oxford, as a Gentleman Commoner.

1840   Breakdown caused by disappointment over Adèle Domecq. Studies interrupted; family goes to Italy for the winter.

1841   Visits Venice 6–16 May, probably staying at Danieli. On return to England completes Oxford degree.

1843   *Modern Painters* Volume I published.

1845   Ruskin's first tour abroad without his parents, visits Venice 10 September–14 October, staying at Hotel de l'Europe (Casa Guistinian).

1846   *Modern Painters* Volume II published. Visits Venice 14–28 May.

1847   Engagement to Effie Gray.

1848   Marriage. Tour of Normandy. Venetian rising against Austrian occupation 22 March.

1849   Venetian surrender to Austrians 23 August. Ruskin publishes *The Seven Lamps of Architecture*. Arrives in Venice for the winter, early November, staying at Hotel Danieli.

1850   Leaves Venice 6 March.

1851   *The Stones of Venice* Volume I published. Defends Pre-Raphaelites and meets Millais. Arrives in Venice with Effie for second winter, 1 September. Takes rooms at Casa Wetzler (now Gritti Palace Hotel).

1852   Leaves Venice 20 June.

1853   Holiday at Glenfinlas, Scotland, with Effie and Millais. *The Stones of Venice* Volumes II and III published.

1854   Effie leaves Ruskin and the marriage is annulled.

1856   Meets Charles Eliot Norton and Edward Burne-Jones. *Modern Painters* Volumes III and IV published.

1858   Meets Rose La Touche. Religious 'unconversion' while on a visit to Turin.

1860   *Modern Painters* Volume V published. Essays on political economy for *Cornhill Magazine* (*Unto This Last*) published.

1864   Death of John James Ruskin. Ruskin's cousin Joan Agnew joins the family.

1866   Ruskin proposes to Rose La Touche.

1869   Summer in Switzerland and Italy, working chiefly at Verona. Short visits to Venice in May, July and August. Ruskin elected Slade Professor of Fine Art at Oxford.

1870   Tour of Switzerland and Italy; visits Venice 25 May–20 June, staying at Hotel Danieli.

1871   First number of *Fors Clavigera* published. Ruskin buys Brantwood, lakeside house overlooking Coniston Water. Illness at Matlock; starts Ruskin School of Drawing at Oxford. Death of Margaret Ruskin.

1872   Summer in Italy. Visits Venice 22 June–13 July, staying at Hotel Danieli.

1874   Hinksey road building project at Oxford.

1875   Death of Rose La Touche 25 May.

1876   Summer in Switzerland, winter in Venice. Arrives 8 September, staying at the Grand Hotel (Casa Ferro); 24 December 'teachings' from Rose La Touche begin.

1877   13 February moves to rooms on Zattere (Pensione Calcina now built on site). Writes first parts of *St Mark's Rest* and *Guide to the Principal Pictures in the Academy of Fine Arts at Venice*. Leaves Venice 23 May.

1878   Ruskin's first mental breakdown. Guild of St George established, with Museum at Walkley, Sheffield. Whistler wins libel case against Ruskin.

1879   Ruskin resigns Slade Professorship. Publishes *Circular respecting Memorial Studies of St Mark's Venice*.

1881–83 Periods of insanity, but work maintained.

1883   Ruskin resumes Slade Professorship.

1885   Resigns Slade Professorship. First section of autobiography, *Praeterita* published.

1887   Further attack of insanity.

1888   Last continental tour. Visits Venice in October. Ill again at Paris.

1889–1900 At Brantwood in the care of Joan and Arthur Severn.

1900   Dies 20 January.

FIG 2 George Richmond *Portrait of John James Ruskin*, 1848.

RUSKIN'S VENICE

VENICE had known a century and a half of tourism when Mr and Mrs Ruskin first brought their only child John to the city in 1835. Venice was not what it once had been – but then, that was part of the romance of the place. In the previous century English visitors had come, ostensibly for educational reasons, as part of the Grand Tour, and the pleasures they had taken there had been set against the backdrop of a decadent but still lively and independent city state. Napoleon ended all that. In 1797 his army demanded the surrender of the city and the resignation of the Doge, thus bringing to an end the history of an aristocratic republic that once had ruled a Mediterranean empire. When in turn the Napoleonic empire was dismembered in 1815, Venice settled down to being a colony of the Austrians. The great days were over.

Tourism, on the other hand, revived. The very fact that Venice had been a great power, and was so no longer, became an attraction to British visitors – subjects of a nation which, like Venice, depended on trade, technological secrets and sea-power for its success, and which, unlike Venice, had survived Napoleon. That attraction was happily reinforced by the fact that one decadent but seductive English aristocrat chose to come to live in the city in 1817. His name was Lord Byron (1788–1824), and being a poet as well as an aristocrat he was able to make something of the splendour and decay he found there – and to draw a moral for the British:

> *... thy lot*
> *Is shameful to the nations, – most of all,*
> *Albion! to thee: the Ocean queen should not*
> *Abandon Ocean's children; in the fall*
> *Of Venice think of thine, despite thy watery wall.*[1]

Mr and Mrs John James Ruskin by no means approved of Byron's private life, but they appreciated his poetry, and encouraged their son to do likewise. They were also familiar with the work of another early visitor to Venice after the Napoleonic wars, the poet and connoisseur Samuel Rogers (1763–1855), who put his finger on that singular feature of Venice which was, and still is, the key to the city's mystery:

Fig 4 John Ruskin *St Mark's from the Piazzetta*, 1835.

There is a glorious City in the Sea
The Sea is in the broad, the narrow streets,
Ebbing and flowing; and the salt sea-weed
Clings to the marble of her palaces.[2]

When Samuel Rogers first published a collection of poems celebrating his post-Napoleonic tour as *Italy* in 1822, it was not a great success, but he later had the idea of issuing an illustrated edition. One of the artists he employed to supply engraved vignettes was J.M.W. Turner. Turner (1775–1851) too, was a post-Napoleonic visitor, in 1819, and on occasion he would use Byron as a text for his own vision of Venice. Turner, and other lesser artists such as Samuel Prout (1783–1852) who illustrated Venice in the popular collections of sentimental poems and stories published in England in the 1820s and 1830s, all helped to prepare the Ruskin family with an image of the city that they would meet. For his thirteenth birthday in 1832 young John Ruskin was presented with the illustrated edition of Rogers's *Italy*. He wrote some fifty years later in his autobiography that this was: 'the first means I had of looking carefully at Turner's work: and I might, not without some appearance of reason, attribute to the gift the entire direction of my life's energies.'[3]

Fig 5 J.M.W. Turner *Venice,* vignette to Rogers's *Italy.*

Fig 6 *(opposite above)*
J.M.W. Turner *Venice, the Riva degli Schiavoni from the Basin of St Mark's,* 1840.

Fig 7 *(opposite below)*
J.M.W. Turner *The Accademia,* 1840.

FIG 8 J.M.W. Turner *Juliet and her Nurse* (engraving).

Both Turner and Venice were to play a central role in Ruskin's life.

The family first saw Venice for themselves in 1835. They had already visited Italy, in 1833, but, beaten back by the summer heat, they had not reached the city. In 1835 they chose a cooler time to travel. In Venice the sixteen-year-old Ruskin had a shot at Byron:

> *I've tried St Mark's by midnight moon and in Rialto walked about*
> *A place of terror and of gloom which is very much talked about,*
> *The gondolier has rowed me by the house where Byron took delight*
> *The palace too of Foscari is very nearly opposite.*[4]

Pastiche can be the sincerest form of hero-worship. 'My Venice' he wrote in his autobiography, 'like Turner's, had been chiefly created for us by Byron' (35.295).

That the Ruskins should be making regular tours of the continent was a sign of the family's increasing prosperity. They were lower middle-class in origin, John James having come down to London from Edinburgh as an unsalaried clerk in 1802. He left behind his father, a grocer trying to establish a superior social position as merchant, his mother and, as his mother's companion, his cousin Margaret. John James had practised a little amateur painting and was interested in literature, but in 1808 his father failed financially,

FIG 9 (*above*) John Ruskin *Notes on Turner's The Sun of Venice Going to Sea.*

FIG 10 (*right*) J.M.W. Turner *The Sun of Venice Going to Sea,* 1843.

and rather than see a family bankruptcy he undertook to pay off his father's debts. He became engaged to Margaret, but it was not until nine years later that he was able to marry her. By then the debts had been cleared, but the debtor had committed suicide after a period of insanity. On their marriage, John James was thirty-two and Margaret thirty-seven, and John, born in 1819, was to be their only child. In compensation for his father's failure, John James Ruskin had risen to become the chief partner in the expanding sherry-importing firm of Ruskin, Telford & Domecq.

One direct result of the visit of 1835 was that the young Ruskin was able to use his topographical knowledge to defend Turner's vision of the city. In 1836 there was some amusement at the Royal Academy's annual exhibition when Turner chose to move the setting of Shakespeare's play *Romeo and Juliet* from Verona to Venice in order to provide a subject for a view of St Mark's cathedral by firework and moonlight. Conservative critics objected both to the idea of Juliet and her nurse being in Venice, and to the 'higgledy piggledy' composite view of Venice which Turner presented. Raised to a 'black anger' by the attack on Turner in *Blackwood's Magazine* (35.217), in reply Ruskin argued:

> it is no such thing; it is a view taken from the roofs of the houses at the S.W. angle of St Mark's place, having the lagoon on the right, and the column and church of St Mark in front. The view is accurate in every particular, even to the number of divisions in the Gothic of the Doge's palace (3.637)

Ruskin's father had begun to collect Turner water-colours, and since he knew the artist personally, John James sent his son's defence to Turner, who asked that it should not be submitted to the magazine. Thus, though a turning-point for Ruskin, this first defence remained unpublished in Ruskin's lifetime. His views were to develop and change before he began his true work on Turner in 1843, but the dynamics of attack and defence were an intellectual stimulus to Ruskin, and his father encouraged his enthusiasm by buying more Turners for the family home.

By 1841 John James and Margaret could be proud of their son's developing interests, as a published poet, as a contributor to J.C. Loudon's *Architectural Magazine*, as an enthusiastic geologist and as a fine amateur draughtsman, but they were also a little worried. They had assured his social position as a gentleman by sending him to study with the aristocratic undergraduates at Christ Church, Oxford, but the rapid progress that might have led to a career in the established church had been halted by a nervous upset. John had fallen in love with Adèle Domecq, the daughter of his father's Spanish – and Roman Catholic – partner in the sherry firm. When she showed no interest in him, he became so ill that his studies were interrupted and hopes of academic success had to be abandoned. To distract their son, the Ruskins took him on a long tour of the continent, which included ten days in Venice.

John Ruskin was now twenty-two, with an aptitude for drawing that had been carefully shaped and encouraged by the employment of not one, but two drawing masters. The second of these, Copley Fielding (1787–1855) was the best that money could buy, for he was President of the Old Water-Colour Society, the leading organization promoting the work of artists who did not paint in oils. These artists learned from the technical advances made in water colour made by Turner, and at times tried to emulate the grandeur and scale of oil paintings, but for the most part they were content with a more restricted view, presenting landscape and architectural subjects in terms of a conventional visual vocabulary of tidy compositions with pleasing effects of texture, light and shade. Ruskin modelled his early drawings most closely on the architectural lithographs of Samuel Prout: Prout's *Picturesque Sketches in Flanders and on the Rhine* had stimulated John James to take his family on their first long continental tour, and Ruskin's early architectural drawings follow in the picturesque tradition. Prout was a personal friend of the Ruskin family, and artist and imitator were sufficiently close for Prout to return the compliment by borrowing one of Ruskin's drawings to copy. (28.756)

In Venice in May 1841 the young Ruskin was happy to fall in with the conventional pictorial view of the city, and to surrender to the appropriate romantic sensations. He wrote in his diary: 'I feel fresh and young when my foot is on these pavements, and the outlines of St Mark's thrill me as if they had been traced by A[dèle]'s hand.'[5] But at the same time there is a hint of a more critical attitude

FIG 11 Anthony Vandyke Copley Fielding *Landscape*, 1829.

FIG 12 Samuel Prout *Casa Contarini Fasan.*

FIG 13 John Ruskin *Casa Contarini Fasan, 1841.*

developing, particularly if his drawing did not go well: 'this place is quite beyond everybody but Turner' (1.447). He was also becoming distrustful of the romantic image of the city created by Byron: 'it now looks as though there had been a slight proportion of what one would call gammon about it' (1.453). This is a foretaste of what Ruskin was to write in *The Stones of Venice* :

> The Venice of modern fiction and drama is a thing of yesterday, a mere effloresence of decay, a stage dream which the first ray of daylight must dissipate into dust. No prisoner, whose name is worth remembering, or whose sorrow deserved sympathy, ever crossed that 'Bridge of Sighs' which is the centre of the Byronic ideal of Venice (10.8)

This later view begins to develop in 1845, a pivotal year in Ruskin's life. Having recovered from his broken heart, Ruskin had set out in 1842 to write a new version of his defence of Turner, *Modern Painters*, the first volume of which, published in 1843, set out to show that contemporary English painters, led by Turner, constituted a school of landscape art superior to all previous schools. He based this argument on his knowledge of English Romantic art and poetry, on geology and natural theology, and on a relative ignorance of the great schools of European painting. In order to continue his defence of Turner in a second volume it would, he thought,

FIG 14 John Ruskin *Interior Courtyard of the Ducal Palace, 1841.*

FIG 15 Photograph of Fondaco de Turchi before restoration.

FIG 16 John Ruskin *Casa d'Oro,*
1845.

now be necessary merely to make a note or two on artists of the past in continental collections, in order to show the inferiority of their landscape painting. Since his emotional difficulties appeared to be over, his parents decided that they could allow their son to travel in Europe for the very first time without them, accompanied only by a servant.

Ruskin's discovery of the extent of his ignorance during this tour was to change the direction that the four subsequent volumes of *Modern Painters* took, and he also began to look at architecture seriously for the first time. It was in truth a general awakening. He encountered not only the 12th century architecture of Lucca, but the tomb of Ilaria del Caretto in the Duomo which became the key comparison for all subsequent discussions of sculpture. He studied the frescoes in the Campo Santo in Pisa, and Fra Angelico in Florence.

In Venice there was another shock: the city was experiencing a period of relative prosperity, and the Austrians were beginning to drag Venice into the nineteenth century. Already the celebrated gondola ride from the mainland, which features in every literary description of the city, had been made redundant by the construction of a railway bridge across the lagoon. For those like Ruskin who still arrived by water, the view was ruined. That first Byronic anticipation having been disappointed, there was worse to come.

FIG 17 J.D. Harding *The Grand Canal, Venice.*

He wrote to his father:

> it began to look a little better as we got up to the Rialto, but it being just solemn twilight, as we turned under the arch, behold, all up to the Foscari palace – *gas lamps!* on each side, in grand new iron posts of the last Birmingham fashion, and sure enough, they have them all up the narrow canals, and there is a grand one, with more flourishes than usual, just under the bridge of sighs. Imagine the new style of serenades – by gas light. Add to this, that they are repairing the front of St Mark's and appear to be destroying its mosaics.[6]

Venice, the romantic city he had celebrated for its melancholy beauty, was being repaired, plastered and painted: 'Of all the fearful changes I ever saw wrought in a given time, that on Venice since I was last here beats. It amounts to destruction – all that can be done of picture now is in the way of restoration.'[7] Ruskin seems unaware of the paradox of his protest: the repairs to Venice were intended precisely as restoration. All he saw was beauty being lost.

Faced with the disappearance of the old facades of palaces like the Casa d'Oro before his eyes, Ruskin tried to record what he could:

> You cannot imagine what an unhappy day I spent yesterday before the Casa d'Oro, vainly attempting to draw it while the workmen were hammering it down before my face. It would have put me to my hardest possible shifts at any rate, for it is intolerably difficult, and the intricacy of it as a

FIG 18 John Ruskin *Casa Loredan*, 1845.

study of colour is inconceivable … but fancy trying to work while one sees the cursed plasterers hauling up beams and dashing in the old walls and shattering the mouldings, and pulling barges across your gondola bows and driving you here and there, up and down and across, and all the while with the sense that *now* one's art is not enough to be of the slightest service, but that in ten year's more one might have done such glorious things. Venice has never yet been painted as she should, never.[8]

The need accurately to record produced another surprise. Beside him sat his latest drawing master, his third, James Duffield Harding (1797–1863), who was also painting views of Venice. But where Harding was content to make acceptable pretty pictures. Ruskin now wanted to understand what he saw. Comparing his work with Harding's he wrote: 'His sketches are always pretty because he balances their parts together and considers them as pictures – mine are always ugly, for I consider my sketch as a written note of certain *facts* … Harding's are all for impression – mine all for information.'[9] Ruskin's study of the byzantine arcade of the Casa Loredan shows the transition between a drawing that explores the texture of weeds and decay to one that is trying accurately to record the capitals and mouldings.

He could not record all that he saw, so he was delighted to discover that the modern world had at least produced one invention

FIG 19 *Daguerreotype of South Side of St Mark's*, probably 1845.

FIG 20 (*left*) *Daguerreotype of the Acre Pillars from the Ducal Palace.*

FIG 21 (*right*) *Daguerreotype of Acre Plllar with Ducal Palace behind.*

that could help him: the daguerreotype.

> Daguerreotypes taken by this vivid sunlight are glorious things. It is very nearly the same thing as carrying off the palace itself – every chip of stone and stain is there – and of course there is no mistake about *proportions*. I am very much delighted with these and am going to have some more made of pet bits. It is a noble invention, say what they will of it[10]

Ruskin, who must have been one of the first art historians to recognise the benefits of photography, began by buying daguerreotypes, but on later visits brought his own equipment, for use by his servant Hobbs. At one time he had more than two hundred daguerreotypes, of which 95 were of Venetian subjects.

As if the destruction of Venice and the rejection of his earlier drawing technique were not enough for Ruskin to be coping with, there was a third shock waiting for him in 1845. He confidently expected only to have to glance at a few pictures by the great Venetian artists like Titian (1487–1576) and Veronese (1528–88) in

FIG 22 (*above*) J. Tintoretto *The Crucifixion of Christ* in the Scuola Grande di San Rocco, 1565.

FIG 23 John Ruskin *Study of the Central Portion of Tintorretto's Crucifixion*, 1845.

order to confirm his opinions about them. Then one day he went to look at the paintings decorating the meeting-halls of a Venetian religious confraternity, the Scuola di San Rocco. There he was confronted by the majestic cycle of paintings by Tintoretto (1518–94). He wrote at once to his father:

> I have had a draught of pictures today enough to drown me. I never was so utterly crushed to the earth before any human intellect as I was today, by Tintoret. Just be so good as to take my list of painters, and put him in the school of Art at the top, top, top of everything, with a great big black line underneath him to stop him off from everybody – and put him in the school of Intellect, next after Michael Angelo. He took it so entirely out of me today that I could do nothing at last but lie on a bench and laugh … As for *painting*, I think I didn't know what it meant until today – the fellow outlines you your figure with ten strokes, and colours it with as many more. I don't believe it took him ten minutes to invent and paint a whole length. Away he goes, heaping host on host, multitudes that no man can number, never pausing, never repeating himself – clouds and whirlwinds and fire and infinity of earth and sea[11]

FIG 24 John Ruskin *South Side of St Mark's After Rain, 1846.*

FIG 25 John Ruskin *Plate VIII from The Seven Lamps of Architecture.*

Ruskin *had* to stay in Venice to copy Tintoretto's *Crucifixion* in the Scuola, the intensity of his response reflected in the vigour of his drawing. He had to draw the architecture, to record as much as possible before he went. In the end he overstayed by twenty days, and his father was both anxious and angry.

Looking back, from the time when he wrote his autobiography, *Praeterita* in the 1880s, Ruskin saw the discovery of Tintoretto as a turning-point. Tintoretto had once said: 'the study of painting is laborious, and the sea always gets wider' (*sempre si fa il mare maggiore*); Ruskin, too, found his subject getting wider and wider:

> Tintoret swept me away at once into the 'mare maggiore' of the schools of painting which crowned the power and perished in the fall of Venice; so forcing me into the study of the history of Venice herself; and through that into what else I have traced or told of the laws of national strength and virtue (35.372).

The effect of this discovery was to make Ruskin return to Venice in the following year, and, as his drawings show, take a new technical and critical attitude to its buildings. His study, *The South Side of St Mark's, after rain* made on 27 May 1846, is still a pleasing composition, but the marble paterae let into the Baptistery wall below the archivolt are numbered on the drawing, the numbers referring to careful notes in his diary. He feared that Venice might disappear before his eyes, for as he wrote to a friend: 'The rate at which Venice is going is about that of a lump of sugar in hot tea.' (36.63) He decided to take a break from the problems of painting in *Modern Painters*, and write a study of architecture, the art not of one individual, but of a whole society. The result was *The Seven Lamps of Architecture*, published in 1849.

Although details from Venetian buildings appear, Venice plays only a small part in the book. The reason was that political events in Europe had prevented another visit after 1846. The revolutions of 1848 stirred the Venetians's memories of their former independence as a republic, and they too rose against their rulers and drove the Austrian garrison out. Independence did not last long, for the Austrians laid siege. Starvation, sickness and bombardment broke the citizens' morale, and they surrendered at the end of August 1849. Such was Ruskin's eagerness to return to Venice, however, that within three months he was back, living among the Austrian officers billetted on the Hotel Danieli.

This time Ruskin brought not his parents, but his wife Effie. Theirs was a strange relationship, for although they had been together since the spring of 1848, when their projected honeymoon in Venice had to be spent examining the cathedrals of northern France instead, the marriage had still not been consummated, and never was to be. Their private feelings about this were concealed from the

FIG 26 John Ruskin
Portrait of Effie, 1848.

world, but there was open conflict between Effie and her husband's parents, for although they had encouraged John to marry they still clung to him as their most treasured possession.

Whatever his private worries, in 1849 Ruskin settled down to a winter of study in Venice, enduring the cold and coping with the shortages created by the recent siege. Assisted in his researches by the resident English antiquarian Rawdon Brown (1806–83), he quickly discovered that the written records of Venetian buildings were contradictory, or non-existent, so he had to evolve his own method. Instead of relying on chroniclers and historians he went to the evidence itself, and methodically drew, measured and annotated. As he explained in the preface to the first volume of the study that resulted, *The Stones of Venice*:

> To my consternation, I found that the Venetian antiquaries were not agreed within a century as to the date of the building of the façade of the Ducal Palace, and that nothing was known of any other civil edifice of the early city, except that at some time or other it had been fitted up for somebody's reception, and been thereupon fresh painted. Every date in question was

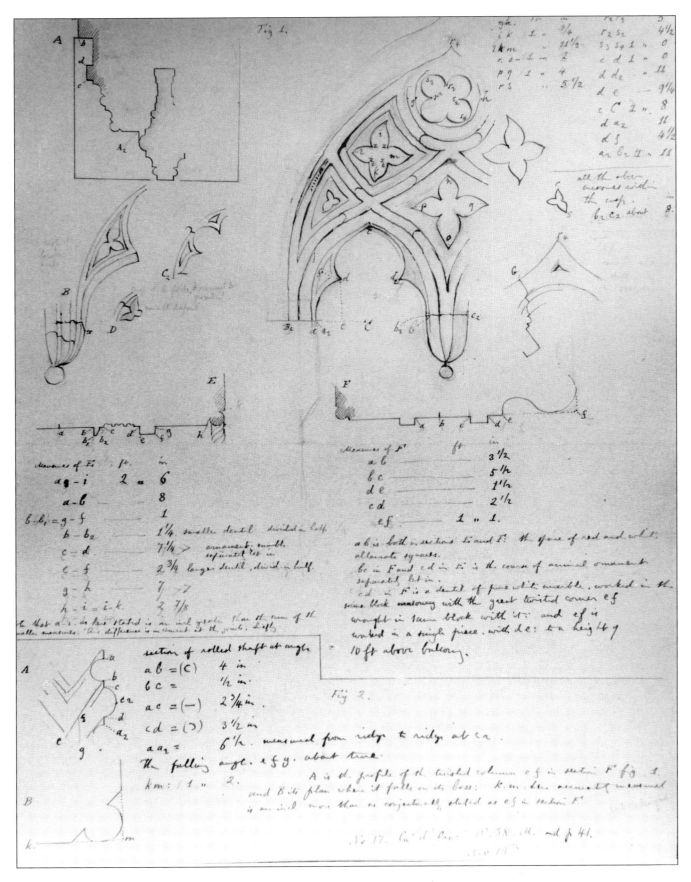

FIG 27 John Ruskin *Worksheet No 17: Notes on the Casa D'Oro, 1845.*

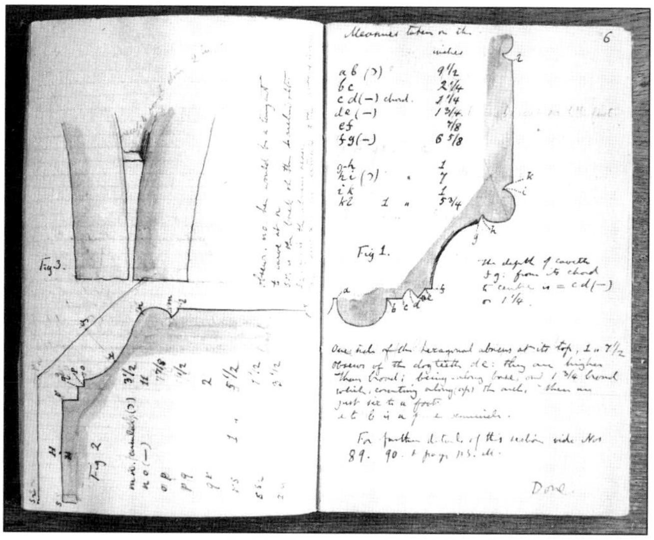

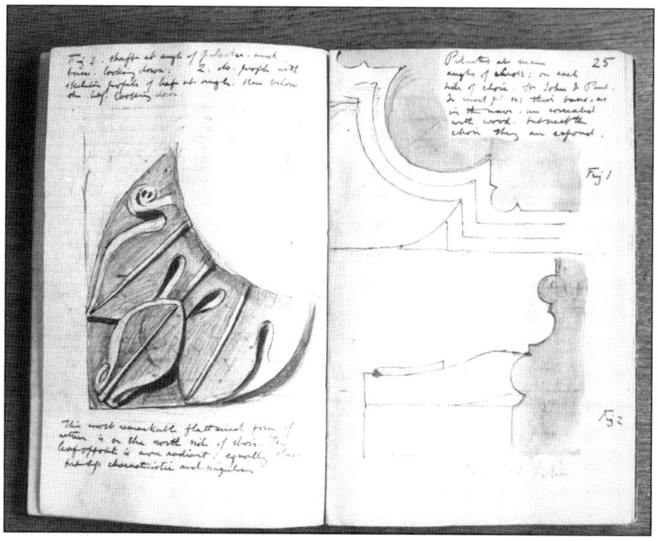

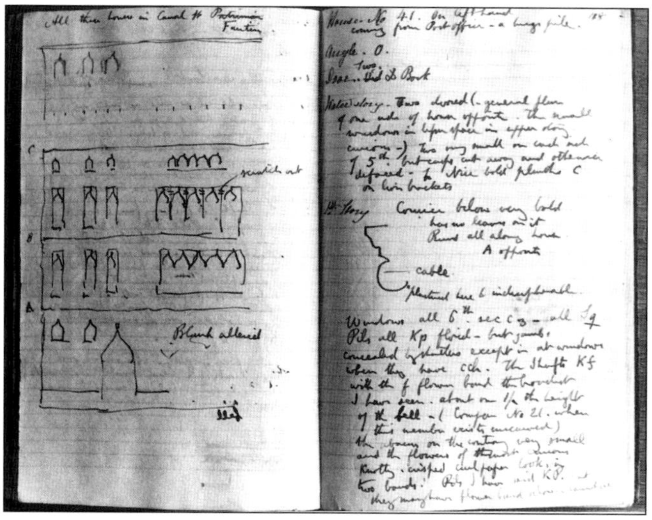

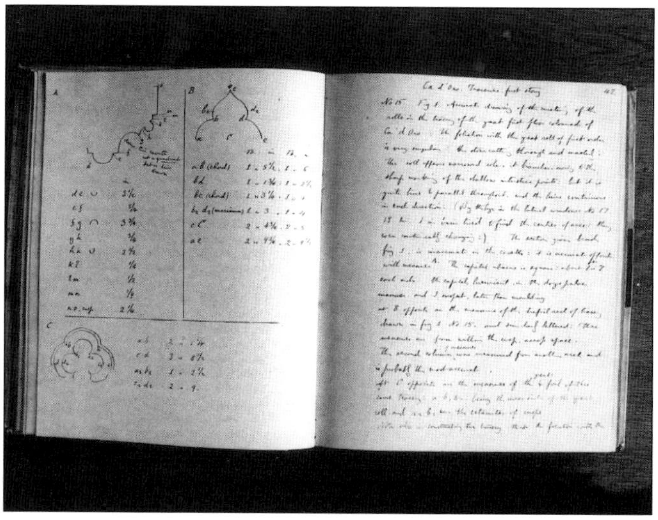

determinable only by internal evidence; and it became necessary for me to examine not only every one of the older palaces, stone by stone, but every fragment throughout the city which afforded any clue to the formation of its styles. (9.3–4)

Ruskin wrote that he had collated most of the written documents relating to the Ducal Palace, but his real claim to authority was that he had also collated 'one document more, to which the Venetian antiquaries never thought of refering – the masonry of the palace itself.'(9.53) This claim is supported by a delightful anecdote to be found in one of his daily letters home, which is set, appropriately, in St Mark's library:

FIG 28–31 (*above*) John Ruskin *Notebooks.*

FIG 32 John Ruskin's Tape Measure.

> Mr Brown recommended me one man as the only one who knew *any-thing* of those connected with the library in the Ducal Palace. I asked him, among other matters, whether the windows, which have now no tracery in them, ever had any. Never, he said – there was not the slightest trace of it. These windows require ladders to get up to them and are difficult in the opening – so it struck me as quite possible that nobody might have taken the trouble to look. Yesterday I went for this special purpose – got the library steps and opened all the windows, one after another, round the palace. I found the bases of the shafts of the old tracery – the holes for the bolts which had fastened it – the marks of its exact diameter on the wall –

FIG 33 John Ruskin
South Façade of the Ducal Palace,
1852.

and finally, in a window at the back, of which I believe not one of the people who have written on the place know so much as the existence, one of its spiral shafts left – capital and all. (9.xxx)

This is how we should imagine Ruskin as he began his research in November 1849; the notebooks and sketches he left behind are a priceless topographical record.

The first fruit of this research was volume one of *The Stones of Venice*, published in 1851. This, apart from a general introduction to the plan of the whole work, was an attempt to lay down a set of universal principles by which all architecture, not just Venetian, could be judged. Another visit would be necessary before the actual history of Venice could be begun. So, with the first volume in the bookshops, in September 1851 Ruskin and Effie arrived back in Venice to spend another winter.

This time they did not stay in an hotel, deciding that it would be cheaper to rent rooms in a private house. Becoming residents as opposed to tourists made for a change in their social status. The Austrians, as an occupying army, had uneasy relations with Venetian society, but the Ruskins could move in both worlds. Ruskin did not like the damage done to buildings being used to house the occupying army, but the political conservatism he had inherited from his

FIG 34 (*above*) John Ruskin *Under the Corner of the Salute* (*Abbazia di San Gregorio*), *c.*1849.

FIG 35 (*left*) John Ruskin *Ponte de Pugni*, 1876.

father meant that he tended to sympathise with the Austrians: 'I never once was able to ascertain, from any liberal Italian, that he had a single *definite* ground of complaint against the Government. There was much general grumbling and vague discontent: but I never was able to bring them to the point, or to discover what it

FIG 36 John Ruskin *Palazzo Dario*, 1845.

was that they wanted, or in what way they felt themselves injured; nor did I ever myself witness an instance of oppression on the part of the Government, though several of much kindness and consideration.' (11.254–5) As he wrote to his father: 'Effie says, with some justice – that I am a great conservative in France, because there everybody is radical – and a great radical in Austria, because there everybody is conservative.'[12] What did make him angry were the guns placed under the arches of the Ducal Palace as a precaution against further rebellion.

Effie, who spoke German, was able to move in the highest social circles; there were garrison balls in Venice and Verona to amuse her, and gallant officers to escort her. (Two of them fought a duel over who should dance with her.) Ruskin was able to enjoy his work, pleased that his wife was being kept entertained. Their routine together suited them both and (though Ruskin was beginning to have doubts about his religious faith) this was probably one of the happiest periods of his life. From his letters to his parents, it seemed as if it was:

> I rise at half past six: am dressed by seven – take a little bit of bread, and read till nine – then we have breakfast punctually: very orderly served – a little marmalade with a silver leafage spoon on a coloured tile at one corner of the table – butter very fresh – in ice – fresh grapes and figs – which I never touch; on one side – peaches on the other – also for ornament chiefly – (I never take them) – a little hot dish, which the cook is bound to furnish every morning – a roast beccafico – or other little tiny kickshaw – before Effie white bread and coffee: Then I read Pope or play myself till 10 – when we have prayers: and Effie reads to me and I draw till eleven: then I write till one when we have lunch: then I go out, and sketch or take notes till three – then row for an hour and a half – come in and dress for dinner at 5, play myself till seven – sometimes out on the water again in an idle way: tea at seven – write or draw till nine – and get ready for bed.[13]

Ruskin was now writing the second part of *The Stones of Venice*,

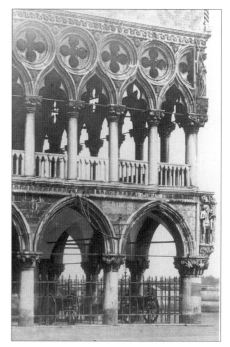

FIG 37 (*top left*) Frontispiece *Stones of Venice*.

FIG 38 (*top right*) *Casa Wetzler*.

FIG 39 (*above*) *Photograph of South-west corner of Ducal Palace, with Austrian artillery.*

FIG 40 (*above*) John Ruskin
A Venetian Gondola (1).

FIG 41 (*above right*) John Ruskin
A Venetian Gondola (2).

FIG 42 Jacopo Tintoretto
*Doge Alvise Mocenigo
Presented to the Redeemer.*
Bought by Ruskin in Venice, 1852.

FIG 43 Domenico Tintoretto
An Allegory of Fidelity.
Bought by Ruskin in Venice, 1852.

and sending it back in instalments to his anxious father in London. John James was anxious because he was always worried about his son, because he was paying for these lavish trips abroad – picking up the bills for Old Masters, daguerreotypes, and plaster casts of sculptural details of St Mark's and the Ducal Palace which John commissioned from an impoverished local sculptor, Giuseppe Giordani – and particularly because he was subsidising the publication of the books that resulted. The first two volumes of *Modern Painters* had been gratifyingly successful, but John's latest productions were not meeting the same response. His father sent advice that sounds like that of a modern literary agent:

> you can only be an author of the *present* day by studying public taste – and for the *future* by writing what is durable – publishers know – Smith [Ruskin's publisher] says the public expected a more pictorial Illustrated Book – full pictures – not fragments – then as to Books no *technical* works are popular or sell – Modern Painters is the *selling* book.[14]

Ruskin found that he had to give up the expensive project of issuing large-scale illustrations to *The Stones of Venice* in a separate part publication as *Examples of the Architecture of Venice*. Many of the technical details he had so thoroughly researched had to be cut out of his text. But over one thing he was firm. There was an important connection between *The Stones of Venice* and his still unfinished *Modern Painters*. His history would show that when the irreligious Renaissance was allowed to get a grip on Venice, Venetian society as well as Venetian art began to crumble. In art, the Renaissance led to the school of classical landscape to which Turner was so superior; in history, it led to the ruin of Venice.

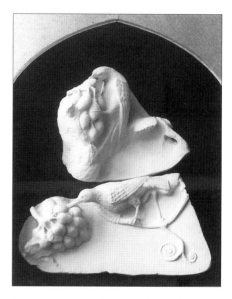

FIG 44 Plaster Cast *Birds in the Vine-Tree angle of the Ducal Palace.*

FIG 45 (*below*) John Ruskin *Façade of the Ca' da Mosto.*

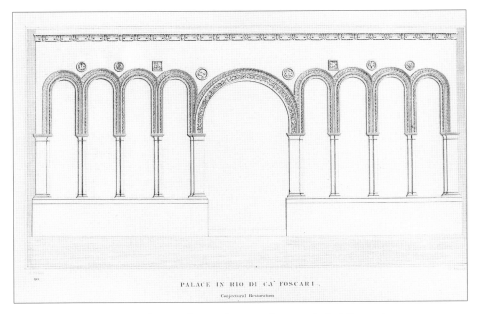

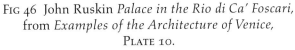

FIG 46 John Ruskin *Palace in the Rio di Ca' Foscari,*
from *Examples of the Architecture of Venice,*
PLATE 10.

FIG 47 John Ruskin *Renaissance
Capitals of the Loggia of the
Ducal Palace,* from *Examples
of the Architecture of Venice,*
PLATE 15.

The key to that ruin was the luxury and paganism that the Renaissance introduced: in Ruskin's view the Venetians turned to the classical architecture of Andrea Palladio (1518–80) – for instance the Church of San Giorgio Maggiore – and the painting of Titian and Veronese when Gothic art and architecture became weakened by an excessive self-indulgence in technical perfection. At first the painters of the Renaissance, particularly Tintoretto, had had a healthy effect, but eventually the Renaissance sank into the luxurious enjoyment of worldly pleasure. This artistic decline was intimately connected with a weakening of religious faith. Ruskin detected a gradual turning away from things of the spirit to things of the flesh in the development of funeral monuments in Venice. This was only one small sign of a general change in Europe which led to the curative but inartistic Reformation in England, and the revival of artistic but irreligious classicism in Italy.

The Stones of Venice is therefore an argument in favour of Gothic architecture at the moment of its purity, and, because he traced the history of the Venetian state from its first buildings on the island of Torcello, Ruskin found himself writing about the Byzantine architecture that had preceded the Gothic. In doing so he was not only helping to change public taste in favour of Gothic architecture as opposed to Classical, he was also effecting a shift of taste within the Gothic Revival as a whole, by drawing attention to the earlier Byzantine buildings, until then generally dismissed as immature and crude.

Ruskin, however, was concerned with much more than public

FIG 48 John Ruskin *South Side of St Mark's,* preparatory drawing
for unpublished plate in *Examples of the Architecture of Venice,* 1849.

FIG 49 C.H. Moore
San Giorgio Maggiore,
1876.

FIG 50 John Ruskin *Torcello:
The Porch of Santa Fosca
and the Basilica behind,*
1850.

taste or the history of architecture. By linking art to the society
that produced it he was going beyond the limits of art criticism, for
he was trying to say something about society itself. The funda-
mental link was religion, but he was also interested in the conditions under which art was produced, and when examining the art
of the Gothic period he was forced to consider conditions of pro-
duction in his own day. The central chapter of *The Stones of Venice*,
'The Nature of Gothic' praised the 'savageness' of the Gothic and
attacked the machine-perfection of 19th century manufacturing:
'It is verily this degredation of the operative into a machine, which,
more than any evil of the times, is leading the mass of the nations
everywhere into vain, incoherent, destructive struggling for a free-
dom of which they cannot explain the nature to themselves.'
(10.194) The chapter inspired the young William Morris (1834–

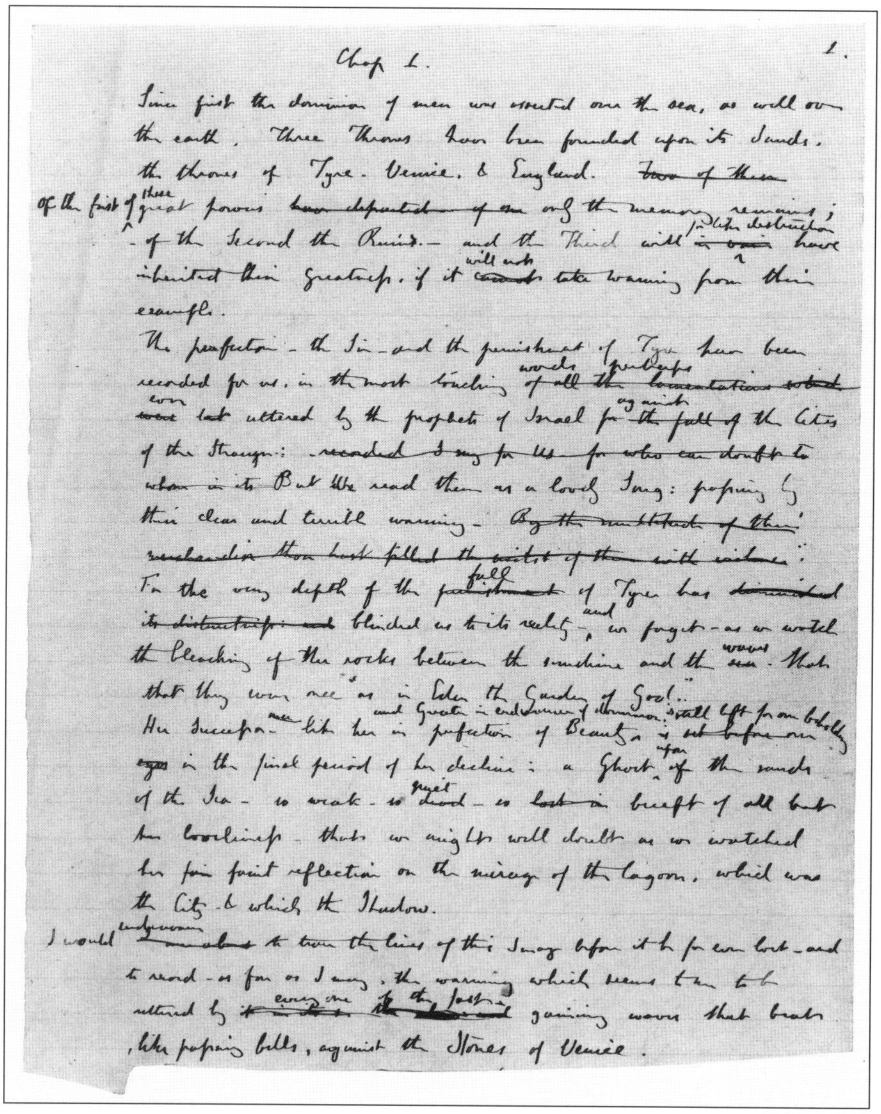

Chap I.

[manuscript facsimile of the first page of The Stones of Venice, in Ruskin's handwriting]

FIG 51 (*left*) John Ruskin. First page of manuscript of *The Stones of Venice*.

FIG 52 (*above*)Vincenzo Catena *Portrait of Doge Andrea Gritti*, c.1528.

96), who was later to publish it separately at his own Kelmscott Press, and it became a founding text for the arts and crafts movement. Ruskin's purpose was political, as well as aesthetic: he was quite clear, from the first time he tried out the opening sentences of the first chapter of *The Stones of Venice* that there was a parallel between Venice and England. (In turn, he saw a parallel between Venice and the ancient civilization of the seafaring Phoenicians, whose city Tyre had fallen to the Venetians in the twelfth century.)

The link which Ruskin established between art and society gave him the great theme which runs through the rest of his writings: that the health of art depends upon the health of society. This was to be the source of his directly social criticism of the 1860s.

FIG 53 J.E. Millais *Portrait of John Ruskin at Glenfinlas,* 1853.

THE COMPLETION of *The Stones of Venice* with the publication of the second and third volumes in 1853 was a significant achievement. It was to be the only large-scale work in which Ruskin carried out what at the beginning he said he would do, even if editorial pressure from his father made him thrust much of his research – what he called the 'dryer or bony parts, in which the strength of the book consists' – into a series of unwieldy appendixes.[15] Having

— 39 —

successfully completed so thorough a study, it is not surprising that Ruskin did not go to Venice again until seventeen years later. (Emblematically, he gave the library of books he had accumulated on Venetian art, architecture and history to the London Working Men's College, where, reflecting his increasing sense of social responsibility, he began to teach drawing in 1854.) Nor is it surprising that in those seventeen years there should have been considerable changes in his life.

The first of these happened not long after the completion of *The Stones of Venice*. In between the two long stays in Venice to prepare the book, Ruskin had met and done much to promote the reputation of the young Pre-Raphaelite painter, John Everett Millais (1829–96). In return, Millais had shown respect for Ruskin's ideas on art, and may have shown him something about the practice of drawing, for Ruskin's drawings in Venice and elsewhere after 1851 show a new attempt at finish. In 1853 Millais and the Ruskins holidayed together at Glenfinlas in Scotland. While Millais painted Ruskin's portrait, the young painter fell in love with the unhappy wife. In 1854 Effie ran away from the Ruskin household and secured an annulment of her marriage on the grounds of Ruskin's 'incurable impotency'.[16] After a barely decent interval, she married Millais in 1855.

Ruskin carried on with his work, especially the completion of *Modern Painters*. The major study of architecture finished, he was able to return to the issue of painting, a return symbolized by the copy from Tintoretto which he made during his last weeks in Venice in 1852. Copying, like drawing architecture, was an intense form of study which enabled him to speak with authority both on what the picture really was, and how the hand that had painted it had been guided by the imagination that conceived it.

In the end, it took another three volumes to complete *Modern Painters*, and when the last volume appeared in 1860 Venice had its special place:

> A city of marble, did I say? nay, rather a golden city, paved with emerald. For truly, every pinnacle and turret glanced or glowed, overlaid with gold, or bossed with jasper. Beneath, the unsullied sea drew in deep breathing, to and fro, its eddies of green wave. Deep-hearted, majestic, terrible as the sea, – the men of Venice moved in sway of power and war; pure as her pillars of alabaster, stood her mothers and maidens; from foot to brow, all noble, walked her knights; the low bronzed gleaming of sea-rusted armour shot angrily under their blood-red mantle-folds. Fearless, faithful, patient, impenetrable, implacable, – every word a fate – sate her senate. In hope and honour, lulled by flowing of wave around their isles of sacred sand, each with his name written and the cross graved at his side, lay her dead. A wonderful piece of world. Rather, itself a world. It lay along the face of the waters, no larger, as its captains saw it from their masts at evening, than a bar of sunset that could not pass away, but for its power, it must

FIG 54 John Ruskin *Study from Tintoretto's Adoration of the Magi,* 1852.

have seemed to them as if they were sailing in the expanse of heaven, and this a great planet, whose orient edge widened through ether. (7.374–75)

There is more to this passage than an excuse to display Ruskin's sonorous prose. He is contrasting the Venice which Giorgione (1476–1510) had known as a boy with the London of Turner's boyhood, to show how profound was the tragedy of Venice when it threw so much away in pursuit of pleasure. Though no longer a strict believer in Protestantism, as he had been when writing *The Stones of Venice*, Ruskin still felt that something had gone wrong when Venetian society lost its moral strength. And, just as Tintoretto had led him to study the history of Venice, the history of Venice led him to analyse the weaknesses in his own society, so that in the 1860s he turned to writing books on political philosophy.

It took some time for Ruskin to recover his appetite for Venice after the arduous work on the *Stones*. He wrote to his new American friend Charles Eliot Norton (1827–1908) in 1859: 'I went through so much hard, dry, mechanical toil there, that I quite lost, before I left it, the charm of the place. Analysis is an abominable business.' (9.xxvii) But, at the end of a long and amusing letter about the pains of research in Venice, he assures Norton: 'I have got all the right feeling back now, however; and hope to write a word or two about Venice yet, when I have got the mouldings well

out of my head – and the mud.' (9.xxix) He considered going there in 1863 and in 1864 made enquiries about the possibility of establishing 'a little bachelor's den' somewhere on the Grand Canal. (36.440) He would have gone in 1866 but for the death of one of his companions on the journey, and the fighting in Italy that, in spite of ending in an Austrian victory, led to the cession of Venice and the Veneto to a United Italy.

When, in 1869, Ruskin finally did return to Venice he feared that the memories of the happy times he had spent there as a younger man would depress him. That year Verona was his main object of study, and he made only flying visits to Venice – by train. He was relieved to find that 'this Venice of mine is far less injured than I feared, and much of it, just as it was, and I have more pleasure in it than I expected'.[17] Part of that pleasure came from his 'discovery' of the work of Vittore Carpaccio (1460–1526), whose cycle of paintings of the life of St Ursula in the Accademia Gallery was to acquire profound personal significance for him in the coming decade. In 1870 he decided to make a proper visit.

Ruskin's father had died in 1864, leaving him a large fortune, and he was able to travel in style. In 1869 there had been official recognition of his work when he was appointed first Slade Professor of Art at Oxford University, so it was as 'the Professor' that he was now travelling. With him were three ladies: his cousin and companion to his mother, Joan Agnew, Joan's friend Constance Hilliard and Constance's mother Mrs J.C. Hilliard. The ladies had a maid, Lucy, and while Ruskin as usual had his valet Frederick Crawley, he also brought along his head gardener David Downes, in order to show him the horticulture of Italy. They stayed, naturally, at the Hotel Danieli. Ruskin had a serious purpose in going to Venice because he wanted to study Carpaccio and Tintoretto in preparation for his lectures at Oxford. He had a scaffolding erected in the Scuola di San Rocco in order to be able to study Tintoretto's

FIG 57 John Ruskin *Riva degli Schiavoni, Ducal Palace and Tower of St Mark's.*

FIG 58 (*above*) John Ruskin
*View of the lower reach of the
Grand Canal, with Casa Grimani,*
1870.

FIG 59 (*above right*) John Ruskin
*View of the upper reach of the
Grand Canal, with Palazzi Corner
and Pesaro, 1870.*

Presentation in the Temple. None the less he and the ladies were happy to behave like tourists, viewing the city by moonlight and, in Ruskin's case, drawing some of its more familiar sights.

What Ruskin was not happy about in these later visits was the *other* tourists who now flocked to the city:

> I can't write this morning, because of the accursed whistling of the dirty steam-engine of the omnibus for Lido, waiting at the quay of the Ducal Palace for the dirty population of Venice, which is now neither fish nor flesh, neither noble nor fisherman; – cannot afford to be rowed, nor has strength nor sense enough to row itself; but smokes and spits up and down the piazzetta all day, and gets itself dragged by a screaming kettle to Lido next morning, to sea-bathe itself into capacity for more tobacco. (27.328)

This publicly stated anger was matched by a private sadness; he told his mother:

FIG 60 John Ruskin *View of the Grand Canal Venice*, 1876.

> I go out and have my cup of coffee in the sunshine, and then sit in my boat, as I used to do with Harding, and draw, not as I used to do with delight, for I know too well now what drawing should be, but with a pleasant sense that other people will have real pleasure in what I am doing. But I don't think I ever heard of any one who so mourned over his departed youth. (20.li)

The reason for this sadness made itself felt very strongly when Ruskin was again in Venice in 1872. This time the Professor's party was even bigger, for Joan Agnew was now accompanied by a husband, the painter Arthur Severn (1842–1931), and besides Mrs Hilliard and her daughter, Ruskin had also brought an artist-assistant, Albert Goodwin (1845–1932). Venice was meant to be the triumphal climax to a four month continental tour, but the visit was spoiled by quarrels among the party – hence the variously glum, angry and embarassed expressions on the faces of the party when they posed for a souvenir photograph. Behind these quarrels were serious developments at home.

John Ruskin was in love. In 1858 he had given drawing lessons

FIG 61 (*above*) Arthur Severn
Joan Agnew in a Railway Carriage.

FIG 62 (*above right*) Photograph of
Ruskin Party in Venice, 1872.

FIG 63 (*right*) John Ruskin
Portrait of Rose La Touche,
1874.

FIG 64 John Ruskin *San Giorgio Maggiore, the Basin of St Mark's and a balcony of Casa Contarini Fasan, 1877.*

FIG 65 John Ruskin *The Zattere, with Chiesa dei Gesuati, 1877.*

to a ten-year-old girl, Rose La Touche, daughter of an Anglo-Irish banker and landowner of strong evangelical convictions and a mother with literary and artistic tastes. Rose was a strange, sick girl, much persuaded by her father's religious views, and prone to episodes of mental instability. The La Touches at first encouraged Ruskin's friendship, but as this turned to love Rose's instability grew worse, while Ruskin's views on religion became less and less acceptable. She once asked him how it could be possible for her to love him, if he proved to be a pagan. In 1866, when she was eighteen and Ruskin forty-seven, he proposed to her. She did not say no, but asked him to wait three years. During these years they were unable to meet, and the La Touches turned against him. Rose's condition did not improve, and her parents sought legal opinion on Ruskin's marital status, which concluded that if he were to marry and have children, the annulment of his marriage to Effie would become invalid. Effie privately added her own bit of spite. In 1869 the anniversary of his proposal passed without an answer, but their relationship was not broken off altogether, falling into an agonizing pattern of brief ecstatic encounters followed by long periods of mutual misunderstanding, and interference from Roses's parents.

In 1872, just as Ruskin was settling down to work in Venice, news came from two of Ruskin's go-betweens with Rose, Mr and Mrs George Macdonald, that Rose was in London and wanted to see him. A telegram calling him home reached him in the Scuola di

FIG 66 (*left*) John Ruskin
Copy of Carpaccio's The Dream of St Ursula, 1876.

FIG 67 (*above*) John Ruskin
Study of the Head of St Ursula in The Dream of St Ursula, 1876.

San Giorgio degli Schiavoni, where he was studying Carpaccio's cycle of paintings of the life of St George. Ruskin hesitated, and tried to persuade the Macdonalds to bring Rose to meet him in Switzerland, saying he could not leave his friends in the lurch. There was a dispute with Joan and Arthur Severn, who left Venice ahead of him; then Ruskin dropped his work in Venice and dashed back with the rest of the party to London, where there was another short, happy interlude with Rose, before another series of misunderstandings.

Rose La Touche died, insane, in May 1875, but Ruskin's obsession with her went beyond the grave. He had already dabbled in spiritualism, and in December 1875 he was convinced by a medium that Rose was attempting to get in touch with him.[18] This experience helped him to regain his faith in an after-life, but it did not bring Rose back. In 1876, exhausted and frustrated by his work as Slade Professor at Oxford, he took leave of absence in order to spend a winter in Venice. He hoped to recover his spirits by spending a long period of work there, just as he had done in in 1849 and 1851. The visit was almost a deliberate reprise of those years, for he was planning to revise *The Stones of Venice* while he was there, in order to remove some of the harsher Evangelical Protestant inflections which he now thought marred the work. In going back over the old ground (for he discounted the hurried visits of 1869, 1870 and 1872),

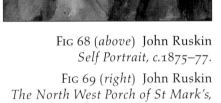

Fig 68 (*above*) John Ruskin
Self Portrait, c.1875–77.

Fig 69 (*right*) John Ruskin
The North West Porch of St Mark's,
1877.

he had hoped: 'the feeling would have been one of exalting and thrilling pensiveness, as of some glorious summer evening in purple light'. But he knew that time was lost: 'To find all the places we had loved changed into railroad stations or dust-heaps – there are no words for the withering and disgusting pain.' (37.204–05)

That pain was inseparable from the pain caused by the death of Rose La Touche. He began copying obsessively Carpaccio's *The Dream of St Ursula*, which he had had placed in a private room at the Accademia gallery so that he and two of his assistants could work behind locked doors. Carpaccio's St Ursula, like Ruskin's Rose, had died a virgin, having told her betrothed, an English prince and a pagan, to wait three years before their marriage. He wrote to his cousin Joan Severn: 'There she lies, so real, that when the room's quite quiet – I am afraid of waking her! How little one believes things, really! Suppose there there *is* a real St Ursula, di ma, – taking care of somebody else, asleep, for me?'[19] That somebody was Rose, and as the anniversary of Rose's first spiritualist 'teachings' approached, St Ursula and Rose began to merge in his mind.

In the view of Jeanne Clegg there can be little doubt that Ruskin 'went through a period of madness in Venice at the end of 1876.'[20] Already in a highly nervous state, a series of chance events encouraged him to believe what he was praying for, that Rose would send him a sign, was happening. In Carpaccio's painting two plants stand on the window-sill of St Ursula's room, on the right a dianthus, on the left vervain. First a specimen of vervain, and then a pot of dianthus were sent, quite independently, to Ruskin by friends. On Christmas eve there came a letter from Joan Severn containing one

FIG 70 John Ruskin *At Venice: Calle del Paradiso.*

FIG 71 John Ruskin *A Street in Venice.*

FIG 72 John Ruskin *Campo San Stefano* 1877.

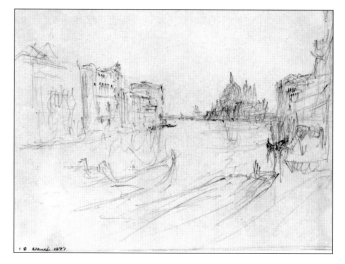

FIG 73 John Ruskin *Grand Canal looking towards the Salute* 1877.

from Rose's mother, which convinced him that he must forgive Mrs La Touche for her actions towards him.

On Christmas day a gift of shells which Ruskin associated with Rose's father were taken as a sign that Mr La Touche must be forgiven too. Ruskin felt impelled to pray in St Mark's and when

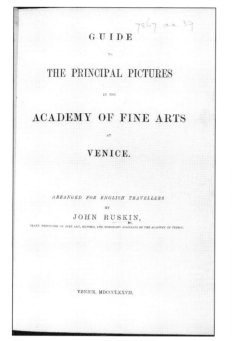

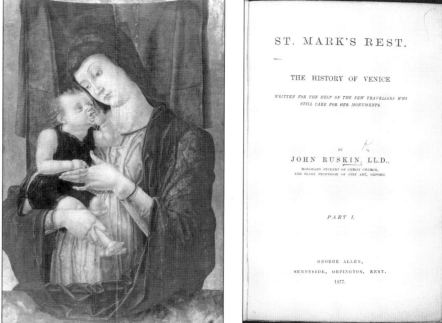

FIG 74 (*above*) Frontispiece *Guide to the Principal Pictures in the Academy of Fine Arts Venice.*

FIG 75 (*above centre*) Antonio Vivarini *Madonna and Child.*

FIG 76 (*above right*) Frontispiece *St Mark's Rest.*

visiting the house of his gondolier later that day the sight of the gondolier's daughter with her baby made him think of the Virgin and child. On leaving he went to the Scuola di San Giorgio degli Schiavoni where he found another image of a sprig of vervain, in Carpaccio's *The Baptism of the Sultan* (another conversion of a un-believer). Ruskin's next destination was the Convent of the Armenians on the island of San Lazzaro, and he went in search of a gondola, only to be confronted by 'a horrid monster with inflamed eyes, as red as coals.'[21] Fleeing this image of the Devil Ruskin engaged another gondolier, but by now the evening fog had come down and they got lost, nearly mistaking the madhouse on the island of San Clemente for the Armenian convent. Later that night he got lost in the fog on the water for a second time.

These experiences left Ruskin in a state alternately of ecstacy and anxiety, his mood shifting violently between exaltation, anger and depression. Both his writings and drawings show the contrast: prose that changes rapidly from serenity to fury; hurried scribbled sketches on the one hand, careful, elaborate drawings on the other. All the time he was working hard; besides keeping up the monthly publication of *Fors Clavigera* (a form of one-man newsletter about his activities) in which he began to hint at the changes that had come over him, he also wrote his idiosyncratic *Guide to the Principal Pictures in the Academy* and, having abandoned the idea of rewriting *The Stones of Venice*, he wrote the opening chapters of *St Mark's Rest*, intended both as a guidebook and a 'fourth volume' to the *Stones*.

Ruskin's literary style had changed, and he was settled into a system of producing his works in small pamphlets which could be

FIG 77 (*top left*) E. Burne-Jones *Study of the Head of Bacchus from Tintoretto's Bacchus and Ariadne.*

FIG 78 (*above*) Photograph of Mosaic fragments of eye of a peacock's tail in St Mark's.

FIG 79 (*left*) J. Bunney *Palazzo Polignac.*

collected up as a book when the series was complete. These series rarely were completed, and *St Mark's Rest* is no exception. Both it and the Academy *Guide* are highly personal, for Ruskin wanted to take his readers round Venice himself, arguing with them as they went. Lunch was included in the itinerary. *St Mark's Rest* begins strongly as he tries to give the essence of his conception of Venetian history and how it could be learned from the pictures and buildings, rather than banal things like political events. Yet his own immediate obsessions distracted him. so that the material becomes disorganized and the reader confused. But then, so was Ruskin. He wrote in a letter shortly before leaving Venice in May 1877: 'I came to Venice meaning to do nothing but finished work! and the lot of scrawls and rags I've done!! worse than ever.'[22]

FIG 80 J. Bunney *The West Front of St Mark's*, 1877-82.

There was however one field in which Ruskin was successful. Since 1845 he had been concerned about the increasing destruction of Venice by the twin evils of of decay and over-enthusiastic restoration. In 1862 he had employed Edward Burne-Jones (1833–98) to copy paintings which he thought were in danger of decay or destruction, and he gradually built up a small team of jobbing artists who could carry out copying commissions for him, not just in Venice, but throughout France and Italy. One of these, John Bunney (1828–82), settled in Venice in 1870; through Bunney Ruskin came into contact with Venetian artists who were also concerned about the way their city was being treated.

They had cause for concern. As far back as 1838 the old mosaic over the central door of St Mark's had been replaced by contemporary work, but the real restorations began in 1857 when the north side of the church was refaced. The south side followed in 1865, and in 1872 the floor of the north aisle of the church was levelled and the mosaics replaced. Bunney gave Ruskin a pill-box containing the pathetic remains of the tesserae that had once formed the eye of a peacock's tail in the floor. Mosaics in two of the vaults were also taken down. There is no doubt that repairs were badly needed, but the architect in charge, Giovanni Battista Meduna (1810–80), whose workmen had been 'restoring' the Casa d'Oro in 1845, made no attempt to conserve the exterior marble facings which, since they were not structural, could have been saved. Instead, Meduna sought to 'regularise' the walls with dull grey marble. When it was proposed that the whole of the west front should be restored (the south portico was already under scaffolding when Ruskin arrived in 1876) something had to be done.

Through the Venetian copyist Angelo Allessandri (1854–?1937) Ruskin met Count Alvise Piero Zorzi (1846–1922), a member of the ancient Venetian nobility who earned his living as a functionary of the Museo Civico Correr. Zorzi was passionately critical of what was being done to his Venice, and had written a book in protest, but was having difficulty in publishing it, either because of lack of funds, or the outspokenness of his opinions. Ruskin, who in the 1860s had helped the sub-librarian of St Mark's, Giambattista Lorenzi, publish documents relating to the history of the Ducal Palace, offered to help, and to contribute a foreword. He wrote an amusing letter home about the trouble he had 'in revising the English with the p[r]inters who didn't know a word of it, and kept changing words all in and out, a sp-litting them in the middle of their ba-ckbones, and making the funniest mistakes in all mee [sic] grand passages at the climaxes.' [23]

The grand passages did the trick, for an enquiry was held and the complete restoration of the west front did not go ahead, though a check on Ruskin's 1850 measurements of the south portico carried out in 1980 showed that columns were moved, and even turned upside down. [24] Ruskin and Zorzi were not alone in their protests, Venetian opinion had shifted, while William Morris and the recently-formed Society for the Protection of Ancient Buildings did much to stir up interest in England – but there is no doubt that the presence and opinions of Professor Ruskin had their influence on the authorities.

AFTER the stress of that winter in Venice, Ruskin did go mad early in 1878, but within a few months was able to go back to work again. When in the winter of 1879–80 he had an opportunity to exhibit some of his pictures in London at the Royal Water-Colour Society, he took advantage of this to make one more appeal for Venice, and published a pamphlet appealing for funds to help with his programme of 'Memorial Studies', copies that recorded still threatened buildngs and pictures. The pamphlet gives a variety of concealing and revealing reasons for his breakdown:

> The illness which all but killed me two years ago was not brought on by overwork, but by grief at the course of public affairs in England, and of affairs, public and private alike, in Venice; the distress of many an old and deeply regarded friend there among the humbler classes of the city being as necessary a consequence of the modern system of centralization, as the destruction of her ancient civil and religious buildings (24.412)

FIG 81 Angelo Allessandri *The Saint introducing the Lion.* Study of detail from Carpaccio's St Jerome leading the Lion.

FIG 82 T.M. Rooke *Christ surrounded by prophets on the eastern cupola of St Mark's.*

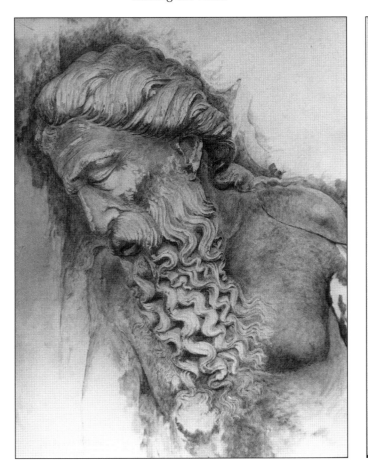

FIG 83 Raffaele Carloforti *The Head of Noah on the Vine-tree angle of the Ducal Palace.*

FIG 84 Frontispiece of *Circular respecting Memorial Studies of St Marks.*

Though he did not go to Venice he still wrote about the city, continuing *St Mark's Rest,* while preparations for an exhibition of his work in America made him go back over his old daguerrotypes and sketches, and make new ones.

Ruskin's 'Memorial Studies' of Venice became part of the work of the Guild of St George. The Guild was his own conception of an

FIG 85 John Ruskin *Moonlight on Venice from the Lagoon,* 1849.

ideal society where work and art would have their proper relation, and people would live together in agricultural communities according to his ideas of social order. Most of the Guild of St George remained a dream, but one solid achievement was its museum, set up in Sheffield to act as an educational centre for the Guild's communities. Many of the copies, casts and photographs commissioned by Ruskin ended up in the Guild Museum, though others were dispersed to other educational institutions with which Ruskin was connected. Some went astray in the general confusion of Ruskin's multiple projects.

Ruskin's mental health was breaking down. There were fresh attacks of insanity in 1881 and 1882, and although Ruskin once more became Professor of Art at Oxford in 1883 his ideas were becoming more and more disparate and difficult to follow.[25] In 1884 he gave a lecture in London which many people found difficult to take seriously. He announced that since 1871 he had been watching the progress of a new natural phenomenon: 'the storm-cloud of the nineteenth century'; the skies were being darkened and the earth chilled by a 'plague-wind ... panic-struck and feverish; and its sound is a hiss instead of a wail.' (34.34)

Some of his audience dismissed this as a sign of Ruskin's madness; indeed, he admitted that his mind was 'capable of imaginative vision, and liable to the noble dangers of delusion' (34.7), yet Ruskin was also right, for industrial pollution had literally darkened England's skies and blotted out Turner's sunsets. Industrial pollution was itself but a visible sign of the moral pollution of the nineteenth century:

> Blanched Sun, – blighted grass, –blinded man. – If, in conclusion you ask me for any conceivable cause or meaning of these things ... Remember,

FIG 86 John Ruskin *Capital 36 of the Ducal Palace, c.*1848–52.

for the last twenty years, England, and all foreign nations, either tempting her, or following her, have blasphemed the name of God deliberately and openly; and have done iniquity by proclamation, every man doing as much injustice to his brother as it is in his power to do. Of states in such moral gloom every seer of old predicted the physical gloom... the Empire of England, on which the sun formerly never set, has become one on which he never rises (34.40–41).

Truly, to Ruskin's harsh disappointment, his audience had ignored the warning of the fall of Venice.

In 1886, after another illness and another recovery, Ruskin made one final Continental tour. Between attacks he was trying to write his autobiography *Praeterita*, and had got as far as 1858, when he first met Rose La Touche. Joan and Arthur Severn were against him telling her story, for the sake of his health, and for the sake of his reputation. This opposition angered him, while to the sadness caused by thoughts of Rose and all that he had lost were added the bitterness and frustration of his public message going unheard. In a pathetic replay of his love for Rose he had proposed to a young art student, Kathleen Olander – and been refused. The storm-cloud of the nineteenth century was beginning to close about him. Ruskin was travelling with a student companion, Detmar Blow, and having received Kathleen Olander's refusal during the journey, by the time he reached Venice he was in poor shape. He wrote home: 'I am a mere burden to Detmar, here at Venice – for I forget all I knew about it – and don't care to – and can't learn it over again – and my old favourite pictures are nothing to me.'[26]

After a few days it was plain that he would have to leave, and he sent a note to his Venetian artist friend Allessandri: 'I am in more pain at going away than I can tell you, but there have been symptoms of illness threatening me now for some time which I cannot conquer – but by getting away from the elements of imagination which haunt me here.' (37.608)

His diary entries are sadder still:

> September 30th, Sunday – but I don't know what is going to become of me.
> October 10th. VENICE. And still less here …[27]

Ruskin broke down in Paris on the way home, and, though he did not die until 1900, a final attack in 1889 ended his working life.

LOOKING back in 1877, Ruskin told Count Zorzi that he was: 'a foster-child of Venice. She has taught me all that I have rightly learned of the arts which are my joy' (24.405). What was it that Venice taught him? There is no questioning the city's importance in his personal life: he visited Venice at least once in every decade of his working career; there were significant changes in his outlook because of what he saw there. His ideas develop from the early, romantic intimations of splendour and decay, through increasing confidence in his powers as an artist and critic, to the point where he can meet the challenge of Venetian art, and write his major work embracing the whole history and culture of the city. Completion of that work marks no break in the progressive study of Venice's art and buildings. Even at the end, when he is overwhelmed by personal difficulties, themselves part of his association with the place, he passes his work on to others, still trying to record the splendour, and halt the decay.

Beyond the unique qualities of 'a glorious city in the sea', where each individual building seemed to contain a work of art, to be a work of art, and to take part in a greater work of art, Venice represented a special synthesis of all the forces which Ruskin believed were at work in art, religion and society. He could see this interaction in every possible mode: the city was set between land and sea and could not exist as it did if it were completely part of either. Its geographical location was poised between the cold north and the warm south, and the tides of Venice (which had a special fascination for Ruskin) had their parallel in the ebb and flow of eastern and western influence. That ebb and flow caused a confluence of architectural styles. Venice was: 'the field of contest between the three pre-eminent architectures of the world: – each architecture expressing a condition of religion; each an erroneous condition, yet necessary to the correction of the others, and corrected by them.' (9.38)

In whatever mode, the synthesis evolved within a concentrated space, a few water-isolated square miles. That *The Stones of Venice* is the most entire of Ruskin's major works is a result of the physical unity of his subject; and, because from 1849 to 1853 he spent the longest period of concentration on a single topic in his life; unity of place coincided with unity of study.

His father, for one, complained that this study concentrated too much on details, that, for instance, the large plates of *Examples of the Architecture of Venice* gave no complete pictures of buildings, only technical abstracts or minute fragments. Yet it was in the details, the pointing of a cusp, the turning of crocket, that Ruskin found the truth he could not find in the chronicles. The hundreds of details in his notebooks each represented a microcosmic view of the whole history of Venetian architecture, and of Venetian society. In *The Stones of Venice* Ruskin began to develop a critical methodology and literary form in which the part stood for the whole, what Barry Bullen has called Ruskin's 'synecdochic method' of cultural history.[28] Ruskin, writes Bullen:

> locates the European-wide conflict of interests at the point of maximum stress – Venice – and he does so in such a way that Venice becomes the 'arena' of the contending forces. Venice, Ruskin claims in a mood of interpretative extravagance, is 'the source of the Renaissance' (9.47), and it is 'the centre of the Renaissance system' (11.82). But that is not all. Ruskin further refines his 'history' away from that of the political historian. Inevitably the history of politics is propelled forward by time and events; Ruskin deals instead with the much slower time of the development of artistic style. Not only are the contending forces located in a single place, Venice; they are focused, as in a burning glass, within a single art – architecture.[29]

As an example of what Bullen has so suggestively termed Ruskin's 'synecdochic method' consider his description of the Ducal Palace as: 'the central building of the world'. (9.38) In his minute examinations of the capitals of the Ducal Palace the capital stood for the building, the building for Venice – and Venice for history. But this synecdoche is also synthesis, for what Ruskin wrote was: 'The Ducal palace of Venice contains the three elements in exactly equal proportions – the Roman, Lombard, and Arab. It is the central building of the world.' (9.38)

Venice became a stage for the interaction of forces which played out a classic, archetypal drama: the tragedy of rise, and triumph, and decline and fall:

> nations first manifest themselves as a pure and beautiful animal race, with intense energy and imagination. They live lives of hardship by choice, and by grand instinct of manly discipline: they become fierce and irresistible soldiers; the nation is always its own army, and their king or chief head of government, is always their first soldier … Then, after their great military period, comes the domestic period; in which, without betraying

FIG 87 G. Bellini *Procession in the Piazza San Marco*, 1496.

the discipline of war, they add to their great soldiership the delights and possessions of a delicate and tender home-life: and then, for all nations, is the time of their perfect art, which is the fruit, the evidence, the reward of their national ideal of character, developed by the finished care of the occupations of peace ... But always, hitherto, after the great period, has followed the day of luxury, and pursuit of the arts for pleasure only. And all has so ended (19.391–92).

Trying to understand the reasons for the inevitability of this tragedy, Ruskin changed his metaphor and presented political history in terms of the ebb and flow of organic life:

> The history of Venice divides itself, with more sharpness than any other which I have read, into periods of distinct tendency and character; marked in their transition, by phenomena no less definite than those of the putting forth the leaves, or setting of the fruit, in a plant ... If we rightly trace the order, and estimate the duration, of such periods, we understand the life, whether of an organized being, or a state. But not to know when the seed is ripe, or the soul mature, is to misunderstand the total creature (24.240).

The rise and fall of Venice was a true story from which lessons were to be directly drawn, but it was also a figure with a much wider significance: 'these two histories of the religion and policy of Venice are only intense abstracts of the same course of thought and events in every nation of Europe.' (24.258) Venice was part of the continuity of Europe, reaching back to the civilization of Tyre, the ancient city which the Venetian navy had helped to destroy in the twelfth century and on whose dominions Venetian power and culture were partially built, and reaching forward to the great naval power of Ruskin's own day: England. This was the primary message of *The Stones of Venice*, and as the sonorities of its opening paragraph proclaim, the story of Venice was a warning for his own time.

Ruskin's ideas of what lessons could be drawn from the fall of

FIG 88 V. Carpaccio *The Arrival of the English Ambassadors, c.1496–98.*

Venice underwent modification in the course of his life. At first confined to the dogmatic Evangelical Protestantism of his parents, he saw resistance to the political power of Roman Catholicism – then threatening to revive in England – as a principal virtue of Venice.[30] After he had first lost his faith and then re-established it on a broader plane, he recognized the 'degree in which all my early work on Venetian history was paralyzed by this petulance of sectarian egotism', and added, with the wisdom of age: 'there are few of the errors against which I have to warn my readers, into which I have not myself at some time fallen' (24.260). Sectarian or not, Ruskin never changed his view that there should be consistency between private morality and public virtue, and that the moment individual self-discipline was surrendered to luxury – especially in art – then national strength was attacked by a fatal weakness.

Study of the conditons under which art lost its moral strength led Ruskin to consider the conditions under which it was created, and to argue that here, too, there must be a consistency of attitude between one man and another, from the humblest worker to the highest artist. Each must have his place and recognition of his status as a man. (Ruskin was at one with his age in according a lesser, yet morally superior, status to women.) Here the parallel with England was clear, for the Industrial Revolution had reduced the mass of men to the status of a machine. To restore the individual worker to his full humanity would mean some loss of mechanical efficiency, but the gain in public virtue would be immense.

Ruskin gradually laid greater and greater emphasis on this aspect of *The Stones of Venice*. His criticism of industrial society has often been misunderstood, since it is similar (having the same subject matter) to the criticisms made by the founders of Socialism; but Ruskin was working from the opposite direction, for he wanted to return to an idealized former state of society, rather than over-turn all and start again. The government of Venice became his ideal: an elected monarchy governing a benevolent and courageous aris-tocracy, who would in turn supervise the activities of a harmonious community of soldiers, farmers, fishermen and craftsmen, all of whom found their collective expression in the artistic glories of the state. Power and consent would flow back and forth from highest to lowest, in an organic relation as natural as Venice's with the sea.

The backward-looking nature of Ruskin's criticism of contem-porary society did not make it any the less biting. And as the con-ditions of the nineteenth century appeared to worsen, and Ruskin's personal disappointments multiplied, the dialogue between past and present became increasingly bitter. So Carpaccio's painting in the Accademia of the arrival of the English ambassadors to arrange the marriage of St Ursula dissolves into a black picture of the present day:

> the orderliness and freshness of a Venetian campo in the great times; gar-den and city you see mingled inseparably, the wild strawberry growing at the steps of the king's court of justice, and their marble sharp and bright out of the turf. Clean everything, and pure; – no cigars in anybody's poi-soned mouth – no voiding of perpetual excrement of saliva on the pre-cious marble or living flowers (24.176–7).

In the end, as the tourists reading Ruskin's guide to the Accademia were forced to recognize, Venice was herself subject to the ruinous pressure of the society to which she was supposed to be the proud contrast.

There had been something noble about the decaying Venice of Ruskin's boyhood – Byron's Venice, when the city seemed to be in a natural process of decline which would allow the buildings slowly to slip into the water, and the land to return to the state of the marshy islands where the founders of Venice had first taken ref-uge. The Venice of Ruskin's old age was one of iron bridges and steam whistles, the buildings destroyed by the act of propping them up. When he traced the process of collapse in society, not just in Venice, but in England, France and anywhere where wealth and pleasure supplanted faith and nobility, Ruskin placed the final stage at 'the reign of St Petroleum instead of St Peter' (24.262).

As the tankers make their way across the Venetian lagoon to the oil refineries at Mestre, what words would Ruskin find today?

FIG 89 John Ruskin *Study of Dawn. The First Scarlet on the Clouds.*

NOTES

1   Byron, *Childe Harold's Pilgrimage*, Canto IV, verse xvii.

2   S. Rogers, *Italy: A Poem*, 2nd edition, London, Cadell, Jennings & Chaplin, Moxon, 1830, p.47.

3   J. Ruskin, *The Works of John Ruskin* (Library Edition), eds E.T. Cook and A. Wedderburn, 39 vols, London, George Allen, 1903–12, vol. 35, p.29. All further references to Ruskin's works in this edition will appear in the text, thus: (35.29).

4   J. Ruskin, transcribed from an unpublished verse letter to Willoughby Jones, 1835. Ruskin Library, Lancaster University.

5   J. Ruskin, *The Diaries of John Ruskin*, ed. J. Evans and J.H. Whitehouse, 3 vols, Oxford, Clarendon press, 1956–59, vol 1, p.183.

6   Letter of 10 September 1845. *Ruskin in Italy: Letters to his Parents 1845*, ed. H.I. Shapiro, Oxford, Clarendon Press, 1972, pp 198–9.

7   *Ibid.*

8   Letter of 23 September 1845. *Ruskin in Italy, op. cit.*, p.209.

9   Letter of 26 August 1845. *Ruskin in Italy, op. cit.*, p.189.

10 Letter of 7 August 1845, *Ruskin in Italy, op. cit.*, p.220.

11 Letter of 24 September 1845. *Ruskin in Italy, op. c it.*, pp 211–2.

12 Letter of 16 November 1851. *Ruskin's Letters from Venice 1851–1852*, ed. J.L. Bradley, New Haven, Yale University Press, 1955, p.60.

13 Letter of 16 September 1851. *Ruskin's Letters from Venice, op. cit.*, p.22.

14 Letter of 11 February 1852. Transcribed from John James Ruskin's unpublished correspondence, Ruskin Library, Lancaster University.

15 Letter of 1 January 1852. *Ruskin's Letters from Venice, op. cit.*, p.119.

16 *See* M. Lutyens, *Millais and The Ruskins*, London, John Murray, 1967, p.230. In *Millais and the Ruskins* the whole story is beautifully told.

17 Letter of 11 May 1869. Transcribed from Ruskin's unpublished correspondence with Joan Severn, Ruskin Library, Lancaster University.

18 For an excellent account of Ruskin's interest in spiritualism, *see* Van Akin Burd, *Ruskin, Lady Mount-Temple and the Spiritualists, an episode in Broadlands history*, London, Guild of St George/ Brentham Press, 1982.

19 Letter of 19 September 1876. Transcribed from Ruskin's unpublished correspondence with Joan Severn, Ruskin Library, Lancaster University.

20 J. Clegg, *Ruskin and Venice*, London, Junction Books, 1981, p.158.

21 Letter of 27 December 1876, quoted in Van Akin Burd, *John Ruskin and Rose La Touche: Her Unpublished Diaries of 1861 and 1867*, Oxford, Clarendon Press, 1979, p.139. The account of events at Christmas 1876 is based on this source.

22 Letter of 20 May 1877. Transcribed from Ruskin's unpublished correspondence with Joan Severn, Ruskin Library, Lancaster University.

23 Letter of 1 May 1977. Transcribed from Ruskin's unpublished correspondence with Joan Severn, Ruskin Library, Lancaster University.

24 J. Unrau, *John Ruskin and St Mark's*, London, Thames & Hudson, 1984, p.55.

25 For an account of Ruskin's relations with Oxford, *see* R. Hewison, *Ruskin and Oxford: The Art of Education*, Oxford, Clarendon Press, 1996.

26 J. Ruskin, *The Brantwood Diary of John Ruskin*, ed. H.G. Viljoen, New Haven, Yale University Press, 1971, p.373.

27 J. Ruskin, *The Diaries of John Ruskin, op. cit*, vol. 3, p.1150.

28 Barry Bullen, 'Ruskin and the tradition of Renaissance historiography' in *The Lamp of Memory: Ruskin, Tradition and Architecture*, ed M. Wheeler and N. Whiteley, Manchester, Manchester University Press, p.56.

29 *Ibid.*

30 *See* R. Hewison 'Notes on the construction of *The Stones of Venice*', *Studies in Ruskin: Essays in Honor of Van Akin Burd*, ed. R. Rhodes and D.I. Janik, Athens Ohio, Ohio University Press, 1982, pp 131–152.

ACKNOWLEDGEMENTS

The publishers wish to thank the copyright owners for permission to reproduce the illustrations listed below:

Ashmolean Museum, Oxford: FIGS 6, 7, 13, 14, 18, 26, 33, 40, 41, 56, 58, 77, 89.

Birmingham Museums & Art Gallery: FIG. 45.

Bridgeman Art Library, London: FIGS 22, 87, 88.

British Architectural Library, RIBA, London: FIGS 72, 73.

By Permission of the British Library: FIGS 37 (CUP4ol il6 TP8370223), 46 (TAB 12226b PL10 83270223), 47 (TAB 1226b PL15 8370223), 74 (7867 aa39 TP 8370224), 76 (10131 1999 TP 8370223), 84 (7812 f2 TP 8371060).

© M.J.H. Bunney: FIG. 62.

Fitzwilliam Museum, Cambridge: FIG. 57.

© National Gallery, London: Fig 51.

By Courtesy of the National Portrait Gallery, London: FIGS 1, 53.

The Conway Library, Courtauld Institute of Art: FIG. 39.

Harvard University Art Museums: FIGS 43, 75.

Mellon Bank Corporation: FIG. 64.

Metropolitan Museum of Art, John Steward Kennedy Fund: FIG. 42 (1910 (10.206)).

Osvaldo Böhm Fotografo Editore, Venice: FIG. 15.

By Courtesy of the Paul Mellon Centre for Studies in British Art and the Tate Gallery, London: FIG. 68.

The Pierpont Morgan Library, New York: FIGS 52 (MA 398–400), 61 (1961.8), 78.

Private collections: FIGS 9, 11, 34, 48, 53 (photograph by courtesy of the National Portrait Gallery, London).

The Ruskin Foundation (Ruskin Library, University of Lancaster): FIGS 2, 3, 4, 16, 19, 20 (Hobbs), 21 (Hobbs), 23, 25, 27, 28–31, 34, 35, 36, 49, 54, 59, 63, 65, 66, 69, 83, 85, 86.

By permission of the Ruskin Gallery, Collection of the Guild of St George, Sheffield: FIGS 44, 45, 79, 80, 81, 82.

Ruskin Museum, Coniston: FIG. 32.

By permission of Somerville College, Oxford: FIG. 67.

South London Gallery: FIGS 70, 71.

Tate Gallery, London: FIGS 5, 10.

V&A Picture Library: FIG. 12.

Yale Center for British Art: FIGS 8, 17, 50.